ADVENTURES WITH
THE VIKINGS

Written by **Linda Bailey**
Illustrated by **Bill Slavin**

Kids Can Press

This book is for my friends Ellen McGinn and Charles Reif,
who have so graciously and generously shared their beautiful Saturna Island home
when I've needed a writing retreat. — L.B.

For Jan,
the only red-blooded Viking in my family, who, like his ancestors,
has explored so much of this marvellous world. — B.S.

Acknowledgments

I am grateful for the help of Dr. Jesse Byock of the Department of Old Norse and Icelandic Studies
at the University of California, Los Angeles, for his expertise and assistance in reviewing the manuscript
for historical accuracy. Any errors or inaccuracies are my own.

Adventures with the Vikings involved the efforts of many, and I thank everyone
at Kids Can Press who helped bring the book to life, especially my publisher, Valerie Hussey;
the book's designer, Julia Naimska; and my editor, Val Wyatt, whose skills and insight continue to
astound me. I also feel extremely lucky to have Bill Slavin as my "partner" in the Good Times Travel
Agency books. His art not only exceeds my expectations — it makes me laugh, too!

My friend and writing colleague, Deborah Hodge, has been a patient and perceptive reader
of manuscripts-in-process, and I once again owe her thanks. I am also grateful to my friend
Anna Koeller for wise comments, great meals and generous dog-walking.

And finally, an enormous thank you to my family — Bill, Lia and Tess. Thanks for pitching in with your ideas,
your feedback, your enthusiasm and especially your great collective sense of humor.

Text © 2001 Linda Bailey
Illustrations © 2001 Bill Slavin

Kids Can Press acknowledges the financial support of the Ontario Arts Council, the Canada Council
for the Arts and the Government of Canada, through the BPIDP, for our publishing activity.

Published in Canada by
Kids Can Press Ltd.
29 Birch Avenue
Toronto, ON M4V 1E2

Published in the U.S. by
Kids Can Press Ltd.
2250 Military Road
Tonawanda, NY 14150

www.kidscanpress.com

The artwork in this book was rendered in pen and ink and watercolor.
The text is set in Veljovic Book.

Edited by Valerie Wyatt
Designed by Julia Naimska
Printed and bound in China

The hardcover edition of this book is smyth sewn casebound.
The paperback edition of this book is limp sewn with a drawn-on cover.

CM 01 0 9 8 7 6 5 4 3 2 1
CM PA 01 0 9 8 7 6 5 4 3 2

Canadian Cataloguing in Publication Data

Bailey, Linda, 1948–
Adventures with the Vikings

(Good Times Travel Agency)
Includes index.
ISBN-13: 978-1-55074-542-9 (bound)   ISBN-10: 1-55074-542-5 (bound)
ISBN-13: 978-1-55074-544-3 (pbk.)   ISBN-10: 1-55074-544-1 (pbk.)

1. Civilization, Viking — Juvenile literature. 2. Vikings — Juvenile literature.
I. Slavin, Bill. II. Title. III. Series: Bailey, Linda, 1948– . Good Times Travel Agency.

DL65.B34 2001   j948'.022   C00-932800-9

It was a dark and stormy afternoon. Thunder rumbled and lightning flashed as the Binkerton twins — Josh and Emma — hurried home from school with their little sister, Libby.

When they reached the Good Times Travel Agency, they walked even faster — and no wonder! Good Times was scary even on a nice day. On the outside, it was dingy and dilapidated. On the inside, it was — downright dangerous. The Binkertons had been inside Good Times before. They knew what kind of travel agency it *really* was.

But as they tried to scurry past, the storm picked up. A sudden blast of hailstones hit the sidewalk, driving the Binkertons right into the Good Times doorway!

Libby, NO!
Don't lean against that door!

JULIAN T.
PETTIGREW
Owner

The door fell open, and there they were — exactly where they didn't want to be!

Julian T. Pettigrew, the owner, was sitting in his usual place.

How nice of you to drop in!

5

Josh and Emma were desperate to leave. But Libby was the kind of kid who just ... wouldn't ... cooperate.

Libby, pleeease!

Thanks for the visit. We, er, have to go now.

6

Meanwhile, Julian T. Pettigrew was rummaging through his travel guidebooks. Picking one out, he stared at the cover.

Go? That's a marvelous idea! Perhaps a sea cruise ...

Wait! I didn't mean — LIBBY! NO!

Julian T. Pettigrew's Personal Guide to the VIKINGS

Before anyone could stop her, Libby snatched the guidebook out of Pettigrew's hands and flung it open. There was a terrible, wonderful flash and ...

Bon voyage!

... suddenly the Binkertons were somewhere else. They were also some *time* else! The only thing that looked familiar was the storm.

JULIAN T. PETTIGREW'S PERSONAL GUIDE TO THE VIKINGS

Welcome to the Age of the Vikings! What a hardy soul you must be to choose this as your holiday spot.

You've traveled back a thousand years to a part of northern Europe that will someday become Sweden, Norway and Denmark (Scandinavia). The people who live here are called "Northmen" or "Norsemen." They're also called "Vikings." To go "a-viking" means to go raiding on the sea like a pirate and — well, never mind about that now. You'll find out, soon enough.

Did you bring some warm clothing with you? The winters here can be very long and cold. What about a life jacket? The Vikings are a seafaring people. Most live along the coast, close to the Atlantic Ocean, the North Sea or the Baltic Sea.

If you're lucky, you might get a chance to take a little cruise.

Atlantic Ocean

Scandinavia

North Sea

Baltic Sea

EUROPE

9

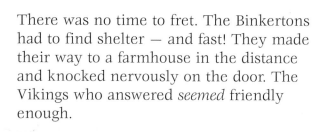

There was no time to fret. The Binkertons had to find shelter — and fast! They made their way to a farmhouse in the distance and knocked nervously on the door. The Vikings who answered *seemed* friendly enough.

Welcome, strangers!

Come in from the cold!

A VIKING HOUSE

If you have a free moment, drop in on a Viking family. They'll be happy to see you. In this harsh climate, people are friendly to wandering strangers. They never know when they'll need shelter themselves.

Most Vikings live in long houses called — guess what? — longhouses. They have to be long to hold all the relatives and slaves who live there. Longhouses are usually made of wood, but stones, turf, clay and peat can also be used.

A longhouse is mostly one long room, although there may be a smaller room or two divided off one end. The long room (or hall) is an "everything" room. It's used for living, eating and sleeping. The floor is made of stamped earth — in other words, dirt. There's a stone-lined hearth in the middle for a fire. (Believe me, you'll need it!) Along the sides are raised wooden platforms filled with earth. They're for sitting and sleeping on.

Does it seem a bit smoky in here? Hazy? Dark? Look around. There are no windows — just a hole in the thatched roof to let out the smoke. The only light comes from oil lamps.

P.S. I hope you like fishy smells. The oil in those lamps comes from fish or whales.

The Binkertons were curious about the Vikings.
The Vikings were even *more* curious about the Binkertons!

Are you a jarl? A karl? A thrall?

Er, my name is Josh.

Have you come far?

You have no idea.

VIKING SOCIETY

By now you have probably met a few Vikings. You may even have found out that there are three classes in Viking society — jarls, karls and thralls.

Being a jarl is great. Jarls are powerful chieftains or war-lords. They own large pieces of land. They organize the karls into fighting bands and lead them on raids.

It's not bad being a karl, either. Karls are free people — farmers, traders, craftsmen, fishermen, hunters. They can own land and carry weapons. They have rights in Viking law.

But if you end up a thrall? Well, bad luck. Thralls are slaves. They have no rights. They work hard doing the worst jobs. Some people are thralls because they (or their ancestors) were captured by the Vikings in a raid. Others are Vikings who couldn't pay their debts.

If you have any choice at all, don't be a thrall.

The Binkertons were soon settled beside the fire, eating a hot meal. The food wasn't bad. But the drinks were a little tricky.

Be healthy!

I give up. How do you put this thing down?

VIKING FOOD

If you like meat, you're in good company. Vikings eat meat every chance they get. Some of it will look familiar — beef, pork and lamb. But you may also see meat you've never eaten before — unless reindeer, whale and seal meat are served in *your* house. Vikings cook their meat over an open fire. They grill it, boil it, roast it or bake it in the embers. They like to eat fish, too. (Very sensible, with all that sea around.) Use your fingers and a knife to eat.

Desperate for vegetables? You should be able to find some cabbage, turnips, peas or beans. There's plenty of milk and cheese, too. And even the poorest Viking can afford flat bread and porridge, both made from barley.

For drinks, the Vikings like buttermilk, ale (a kind of beer) and mead (a drink made with honey). Try drinking the Viking way — out of a hollowed-out cow's horn. You can't put it down, so you have to drink the whole horn-full in one swallow. Now *that's* a big gulp!

The Vikings were very hospitable. They invited the Binkertons to spend the night — and to help out with chores the next morning. Josh was given a job outside ...

How come we always end up on a farm?

... while Emma helped the women with their spinning and weaving. At least, she *tried* to help.

Sorry. I seem to have a small tangle here.

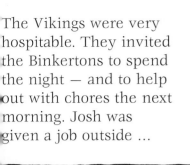

VIKING WORK

Maybe you've heard stories about the Vikings being wild pirates of the northern seas? The truth is — most Viking men spend most of their time farming. They grow crops such as barley, rye and oats. In cold, mountainous areas, they graze cattle and sheep.

Viking men do a lot of fishing, too. In fact, it's sometimes hard to tell whether a Viking is a farmer-with-a-fishing-boat or a fisherman-with-a-farm. Some Vikings are even hunters-with-fishing-boats-and-farms. In northern areas, they hunt reindeer, elk, bears, wild boars, seals and whales.

Viking women farm, too. They milk the goats, sheep and cows and make butter and cheese. They also cook the family's food, bake the bread and brew the ale.

Another important job is cloth-making. There are no malls here, so Viking women have to start from scratch. That means wool, straight from the sheep. First the women clean it and get the grease out. Next they comb, spin and dye it and weave it into cloth. Then they cut the cloth and sew it and — whew! Besides their families' clothing, the women also have to sew sails for the boats — even tents! If you have any time to spare, please give them a hand.

13

When the Binkertons heard that their host was going to "a Thing," they got very excited. They had no idea what a Thing was, but any Thing was better than the farm. That night, while the Vikings slept, Emma and Josh tried to guess.

What kind of thing?

I don't know.

Well, why didn't you ask?

I did. He said it was a special thing.

AT HOME WITH THE VIKINGS

Always remember that you're a guest here. Guests do their best to fit in. So when bedtime comes, don't expect your own bedroom. In fact, don't expect a bed at all. Just find a feather quilt or a sheepskin and pick a spot on the wooden platform along the wall. Maybe you can nab part of a straw mattress — but for goodness sake, move over! The rest of the household, including thralls and distant relatives, will be bunking down with you.

There *is* a small, private bed-closet available, but don't even think about it. It's for the master and mistress of the house. (Who wants to sleep in a closet, anyway?) If you want a bath, ask politely if there's a bath-house (like a sauna) on the farm. The Vikings like to bathe regularly — about once a week. Need to use the toilet? Look for a simple earth pit, just off the main hall, or outside.

P.S. Don't worry about flushing.

The next morning, the Binkertons were on their way to the Thing.

(Whatever *that* was.)

TRAVELING BY LAND

The Vikings are great travelers, by land and by sea. On land, they use horses, at least during the summer months. What a fine animal the horse is! You can ride it. You can hitch it to a cart. You can pile your belongings on it. If you get hungry enough, you can even *eat* it! (Yes, the Vikings do eat horse meat.)

But what about the winter when it snows? Try a sled. If you don't have one, just add skis to your Viking cart and — instant sled! Or put on a pair of skis yourself. The Vikings make skis out of animal bones. They make skates (which they call "ice-legs") out of bone, too, and they use spiked sticks to push themselves along.

VIKING CLOTHING

Want to be in fashion in the Age of the Vikings? Here's how:

If you're a woman, put on a long dress of wool or linen with a shorter dress over top. Use two big oval-shaped brooches to hold up your over-dress. Drape chains of beads from the brooches. Then hang things like scissors, needles, knives, and combs from the chains. (Not quite as good as pockets, but they do the job.) Wear a shawl or cloak over top. Still not warm enough? Line your cloak with fur.

If you're wealthy, put on arm-rings or neck-rings made of silver or gold. These are as good as money. They're made in standard weights and can be cut into pieces and spent like coins.

If you're a man, wear pants — straight-legged, baggy or tight-fitting. You'll need a tunic (long shirt), too. Fasten a belt around your waist. Pop quiz question: Why do Viking men wear their cloaks pinned on the right shoulder? Answer: To keep their sword arms (right arms) free. You never know when you'll need your sword arm — especially if you're a Viking.

What do Viking children wear? The same things as their parents, only smaller.

17

The Thing turned out to be a big gathering of Vikings. It was a lot more interesting than the farm — especially when the Vikings held a trial.

For burning Olaf's house down, you are banished for three years. Go now from this land!

A VIKING THING

What kind of thing is a Viking Thing?

It's an outdoor assembly of all the free men of the district who own a certain amount of property. They meet to make laws and to punish law-breakers. They can also elect chieftains and kings.

The voting is easy. To vote "yes,"

just rattle your weapons together. Do it loudly so that everyone will hear.

Viking laws aren't written down, so somebody has to remember them. That's why they have the law-speaker, a man who memorizes all the laws and shouts them out loud for everyone to hear.

But Olaf started it.

Pah! I still say he should be stoned.

Or at least stick his hand in boiling water.

They don't kid around at these Things, do they?

VIKING FEUDS & PUNISHMENTS

When Vikings get into a fight, their families get involved, too. They start fighting. They set each other's houses on fire! They even start killing each other!

These family feuds can be settled at the Thing. Each family tells its side of the story and brings along friends to say they are right. The judges sometimes test people's honesty by having them snatch stones out of boiling water. (Someone who is telling the truth won't be hurt ... or so the Vikings believe.) Quarreling men may also choose to fight a duel.

The judges set punishments. One Viking punishment is "blood money" (paid by one feuding family to another when someone has been killed). Other punishments include tarring, whipping, stoning and banishment (being sent out of the country). One of the worst punishments is being outlawed. Outlaws are not considered people. Anyone is allowed to kill them.

Not everything at the Thing was serious. There was time for fun, too.

Viking fun.

Sometimes it got a little rough.

This is worse than hockey!

VIKING ENTERTAINMENT

A Thing usually lasts for several days, or even longer. Bring the whole family along and have a camp-out. When the spear-rattling is over, you can join in some Viking sports. Be warned, though. The Vikings think of sports as training for battle. The more violent, the better!

In the swimming contest, for example, it's not how fast you are that counts. It's how tough you are. Forget the butterfly stroke. Just grab your opponent and hold him underwater. When he collapses — or drowns! — you win.

But maybe you'd rather try a wrestling match. Better think twice! By the end of the match, you and your opponent will both be bloody

and bruised. (Even board games end up in blows around here.)

Still interested in Viking sports? Check out the horse fights. The Vikings let two stallions loose at one another and goad them with sticks. The stallions fight to the death while the Vikings cheer and make bets. You can also watch bareback horse races. The riders don't just whip their horses — they whip each other, too!

If Viking sports are too rough for you, join the crowd around the story-teller. He or she will entertain you with tales of gods and kings and brave heroes. Viking stories (sagas) aren't written down. They're learned by heart and passed on to new generations by being told over and over.

Oh, my gosh!
He's drowning
him!

But the strangest sight
of all was the Berserker.

Grrrr!

THE BERSERKER

If you want to meet a scary guy, say
hello to the Berserker.

Notice his outfit? The word
"berserk" means bearskin. Berserkers
are the most feared of all Viking
warriors. Before going into battle,
they get into a fighting rage. They
howl like wolves. They leap like
dogs. They grind their teeth and
bite the edges of their shields.

In battle, they fight with a fury
that's terrible to see. They get into
such a wild frenzy, they believe they
can't be hurt — not even by a sword
or fire. Have you ever heard the
expression "going berserk"? Where
do you think it came from?

If you see a Berserker coming,
walk the other way. Quickly!

hat guy is
angerous!

Yes! Isn't he
wonderful?

Many of the Vikings had come to the Thing on fierce-looking longships. One morning, Josh woke up early and snuck off to get a closer look.

A VIKING LONGSHIP

One thing you must see while you're visiting the Vikings is a longship. The Vikings are superb ship-builders, and the longship is a marvel of its time.

Take a look at the carved dragon on the prow. Does it make you nervous? Good! It's supposed to. A longship is a warship. Scaring people is part of the point!

Surprising people is important, too. Viking ships can travel great distances, to places where no one expects them. They arrive suddenly — and they're usually not welcome!

Wow!

Look at the shape of this ship. Notice how long and low and narrow it is. It's light, too, and very strong. It's a combination sailboat and rowboat. If there's a good wind, its large rectangular sail will whip it along. If there's no wind, it can be rowed with 15 to 30 pairs of oars. Each rower sits on a sea chest filled with his possessions. There's also a steering oar toward the back.

Best of all, a longship is extremely fast. In fact, it's among the fastest ships ever built — until the invention of the power boat.

Wouldn't it be great to take a cruise on a Viking "dragon ship"?

23

25

Meanwhile, back at the Thing, Emma was just waking up. When she couldn't find her brother or sister, she started to ask around.

Then she discovered that one ship had not yet left. It was in the harbor and would set out next morning. That night, under cover of darkness, Emma took a swim.

Emma *almost* got it right. Her ship did set out next morning.

Unfortunately, it was the wrong kind of ship — a cargo ship — and it was heading in a completely different direction.

Iceland? We're going to Iceland?

You will like Iceland.

Only for three years — until Thorvald's banishment ends.

I still say Olaf started it.

VIKING EXPLORERS & SETTLERS

The Vikings are a bold, roving people. They like to explore and settle in faraway places. Sometimes they attack the people who live there and grab their land. Sometimes they fit in peacefully, without a fuss. And sometimes they settle in lonely places where hardly anyone has tried to live before. Viking settlers travel in cargo ships, which are wider and slower than longships and can carry bigger loads.

These settlers end up living all over the map. Some make their homes in parts of Europe and Russia. Others settle farther from home — in Iceland and Greenland. Most amazing of all, some Vikings cross the Atlantic Ocean, all the way to North America! (They don't call it North America. Discovering some vines there, they call it "Vinland.")

North America is a nice place, but the Vikings don't stick around. The native people who are already there (called "skraelings" by the Vikings) don't much care for the newcomers. They give the Vikings a very hard time. After a while, the Vikings leave. They don't come back.

Five hundred years later, Christopher Columbus will finally get around to crossing the Atlantic Ocean. He will *think* he's the first European to reach these shores. If only he knew ...

27

She gobbled down dried fish for her dinner, and at night she was happy to sleep in the open.

Unnnhhhh.

Him, I *don't* like.

LIFE ON A VIKING SHIP

Expecting a luxury cruise? Forget it. Life on a Viking ship is cold, cramped and uncomfortable. You'll probably be damp and chilly most of the time. Seasick, too.

If you're not too busy throwing up, try some longship food. It's likely to be cold and nasty. Fires on a ship are dangerous, so unless there's a chance to land and build a fire, the Vikings make do with dried fish and dried or pickled meat. For a treat, try hard-baked bread and sour butter.

At night, you'll sleep outside on the open deck. Find a leather sleeping bag and snuggle in. (Hint: If you have to share your bag, try not to share with the Berserker.)

In your free time, you'll be working. Viking ships are great, but they have a few little problems — like leaking at the seams. Want to stay afloat? Start bailing.

Most important of all, don't complain. Act tough and bold, whether you feel that way or not. The Vikings admire kids who show spirit — even kids who are aggressive and start fights. If you want the Vikings to like you, *don't* behave yourself!

After several days, the Viking longships reached their destination — a small village with a monastery nearby. With a swiftness that startled the Binkertons, the ships slipped into shore.

Land?

GRRRRR!

VIKING WEAPONS & ARMOR

If you take a Viking cruise, there's a good chance you'll end up in a raid. Be prepared! A Viking warrior never goes raiding without:

- A sword. Use it for hacking and slashing. Hold it in your right hand and dodge, twist and duck as you fight. If you like, you can give your sword a pet name. (Hint: Fluffy and Snookums are not good names.)
- An ax. The biggest kind is a broad ax. Even a grown man needs two hands to wield it.
- Spears. One kind is for throwing. Another is for thrusting, when you're close to your enemy.
- A bow and arrow. These are useful at a distance, but useless close up.

It took Josh a few minutes to figure out what was happening. The Vikings were going on a raid! And they expected him to join them!

OW-OW-OWWWWWW!

Stop! Hang on a sec! Can't I just watch from the ship?

• A shield. This is an extremely important piece of equipment. Remember, while you're busy hacking and slashing at your enemy, he'll be busy hacking and slashing back! Move your shield around quickly to ward off blows.

• A helmet. This is small and either round or pointed. Try to get one with a nose guard — unless you think you'd look better with your nose chopped off.

• Armor. A chainmail shirt is best but very expensive. Make do with a padded leather jerkin. If you're lucky, the layers of leather will keep you from getting too badly hurt.

And speaking of getting hurt, do you really want to do this? Maybe you'd better leave now. In fact, maybe you'd better not even go on a cruise.

Or … maybe it's already too late?

The Vikings behaved very badly on the raid. They stole, burned, looted and took prisoners. Josh was shocked.

Fortunately, he missed most of it.

Fainted!

He doesn't know how to have fun.

A VIKING RAID

Don't go on a Viking raid unless you have nerves of steel.

The Vikings are feared all over western Europe for their surprise attacks by sea. When they leave their homes and farms and "go a-viking," they become fearless pirates, out to win riches and glory in faraway lands. They come out of nowhere! At least, that's how it feels to their victims. Their longships are designed for sudden, sneak attacks. A longship can swoop right onto a beach, allowing the Vikings to leap off and race into a village or monastery with almost no warning.

And what do they do when they get there?

They rob! They grab food, grain, cattle, money, wine, jewelry — whatever they can find. What they can't steal, they burn! Monasteries are especially rich targets, filled with religious treasures decorated with gold, silver and jewels. Monasteries are easy to attack, too, with only a few churchmen to defend them.

If you're being raided by Vikings, here are a few words of advice — RUN FOR YOUR LIVES! The Vikings kill people who resist them. They take captives, too — that's how they get slaves. (If they capture a rich person, they might hold her or him for a ransom instead.)

All over Europe, people are terrified of the Vikings. Some are so scared they *pay* the Vikings to stay away! This payment is called Danegeld.

But before you think too badly of the Vikings, keep in mind that they aren't the only ones looting and burning. Other people are doing it, too.

It's just that the Vikings are so *good* at it.

The ships headed home with their loot.

But before very long, the sky turned dark as night. The wind picked up to hurricane force. Soon the Vikings — and Josh and Libby and the prisoners — were in the midst of a storm so terrible that even the Berserker looked worried.

VIKING RELIGION

When a Viking gets into trouble on the sea, he is likely to call out to Thor, the god of thunder. According to Viking belief, Thor rumbles across heaven in a goat cart, carrying a hammer shaped like a thunder bolt.

Thor is popular among sailors, but he's not the only Viking god. The Vikings believe in many gods who have different areas of responsibility.

One Viking god is Odin (or Woden). He's Thor's father. He's also the god of war, death and wisdom. You might find him a little strange — he has only one eye and rides an eight-legged horse. But Viking chieftains and warriors think he's swell. They believe that if they die bravely in battle, they will join Odin in a golden hall called Valhalla, where they'll spend their time fighting and feasting, just as they did in life.

Odin's wife, Frigga, is the goddess of marriage and the household. Notice a little pattern here? Wednesday (Woden's Day). Thursday (Thor's Day). Friday (Frigga's Day). Eventually the Vikings will become Christians, and these gods will be forgotten. But their names will live on — in the English calendar.

The storm raged over a wide area — wide enough to pick up Emma's ship and blow it far off course.

If I *get* out alive, I am *never* leaving my bedroom again.

VIKING NAVIGATION

It's not easy to find your way around the ocean in the Viking Age. The compass hasn't been invented yet. There are no charts or instruments either, and certainly no radar. Yet the Vikings manage to sail amazing distances — even all the way across the Atlantic Ocean. How do they find their way?

To navigate like a Viking, here's what you do:

• Whenever possible, stay in sight of land. Watch for landmarks you recognize.

• Watch the sky. Pay attention to the position of the stars and the sun. Observe the clouds.

• Watch the sea. Check the color and movement of the current.

• Watch the sea life. Fish, birds and sea creatures can give you clues to where you are.

• Feel the wind. Notice its warmth and direction.

There! You should have no problem finding your way ... unless you get into a storm. If that happens, ignore everything you've just read. You're in *way* too much trouble to waste time watching birds.

Forget navigation! Just hang on!

The next day, the Binkertons got their first lucky break since leaving home. The winds that had tossed Emma's ship off its course also blew the longships off *their* course.

It was like a miracle. The ships were blown together!

It's Thorvald's ship.

I thought he was going to Iceland!

The one in the middle — isn't that — ?

EM-MA!

The Binkertons on both boats begged and pleaded, but it was no use. The Vikings refused to bring the ships alongside each other.

Home is Iceland now.

Pleeeeeease! It's my only chance to get home!

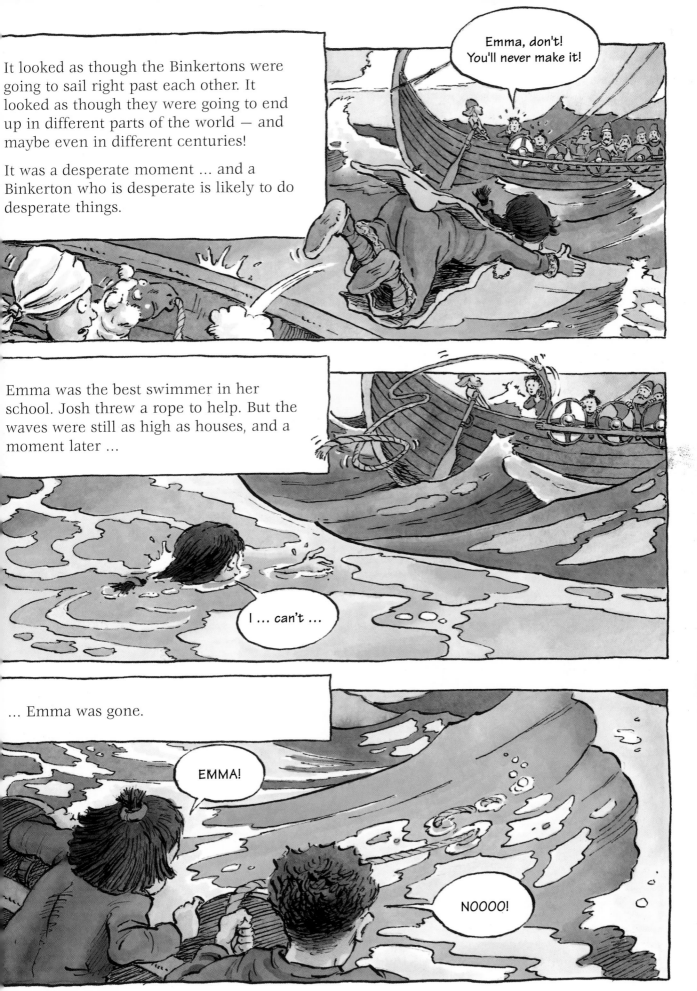

It looked as though the Binkertons were going to sail right past each other. It looked as though they were going to end up in different parts of the world — and maybe even in different centuries!

It was a desperate moment ... and a Binkerton who is desperate is likely to do desperate things.

Emma, don't! You'll never make it!

Emma was the best swimmer in her school. Josh threw a rope to help. But the waves were still as high as houses, and a moment later ...

I ... can't ...

... Emma was gone.

EMMA!

NOOOO!

Yes. Gone.

But not for long. When the Vikings pulled in the rope ... they pulled in a Binkerton, too!

The Vikings were very impressed with Emma's bravery.

She is fearless!

She is brave!

Jus a V

But when Emma heard about the raid, she showed a different kind of courage.

You burned their houses? You're turning them into slaves?

After a few hours of this, the Vikings started to get a little tired of Emma — and the other Binkertons, too. Who *were* these kids, anyway?

Maybe they were thralls.

The Binkertons were in a bad situation. But at least they had a way out.

Before very long, they sailed into a harbor. The kids got a glimpse of a Viking town — but only a glimpse.

VIKING TOWNS & TRADE

When your cruise is finished, why not call in at a Viking town? Towns are centers for crafts and trading.

Stroll down the wooden streets and look for craftsmen. Maybe you'll pick up a souvenir or two. You might see jewelers or glassmakers or carvers of soapstone and reindeer antlers. There'll also be carpenters making spoons, bowls, beds, tables, chests and ... well, you get the idea.

You'll also see plenty of traders in a town. The Vikings are almost as fond of trading as they are of raiding! In fact, a town market is a chance for them to trade some of the things stolen on their raids (including slaves). Vikings also travel to faraway lands to trade. They carry products from their own lands (such as furs, bearskins, reindeer hides and soapstone) and trade them for things they don't have (such as salt, silk, pottery, and wine).

With all these valuable goods being traded, Vikings are careful to build their towns in safe places where enemies can be seen approaching. Notice the rampart (wide bank of earth) with the tall wooden palisade (fence) and towers on top. These are for defense against attack.

Of course, you'd have to be *very* fierce and brave to attack the Vikings.

41

Most of the Viking raiders went off to trade their stolen loot. The Berserker was put in charge of the thralls, who were to be sold later at the market.

It would have been a perfect opportunity for the Binkertons to finish the Guidebook …

… if the Berserker hadn't chosen that particular moment to learn how to read.

HEY!

Grrrrr!

There was nothing to do ... and that's exactly what the Binkertons did.

Why can't we ever go on an *easy* holiday?
Mom and Dad must be worried sick.

The Viking Alphabet

If you are thinking of showing this Guidebook to a Viking, forget it! The Vikings do have an alphabet, but it looks nothing like yours – and not all Vikings can read it, anyway.

The Viking alphabet is called the futhark, and the letters are called runes. There are 16 runes. They look like this:

ᚠ ᚢ ᚦ ᚬ ᚱ ᚴ ᚼ ᚾ ᛁ ᛅ ᛋ ᛏ ᛒ ᛘ ᛚ ᛦ

Notice how straight the lines are, and how they're mostly up-and-down or slanted. That's because runes are meant to be carved in wood, and it's hard to carve curvy letters. Runes are also carved in stone, bone and metal. (The Vikings don't have paper.)

There are some good things about writing in runes. All you need is a stick to carve your message on and a knife to cut with. Made a mistake? No problem. Just cut out that part of the stick.

The bad thing about writing in runes is – how do you write a long message on a stick?

The Vikings use runes in different ways. They send carved messages to each other. They describe their brave deeds in runes on large standing stones. They also believe runes can be used to cast magic spells – to protect someone in battle, for example, or to cure illness.

The situation looked bleak. But the Binkertons were not the kind of kids who gave up easily. Emma waited and watched. The moment she saw her chance, she took it!

It wasn't easy to get a large group of sleepy, tied-up thralls to move together.

But eventually the Binkertons were where they wanted to be — close enough to the Berserker to read the Guidebook.

Perfect! It's open to the last page. Libby? Josh? READ!

Emma and Josh and Libby read the final words of the Guidebook — the words that would take them forward through time. Emma reached over to close the book and ...

... the Binkertons were home.

And it looked as though they'd brought a few friends with them!

Oh ... my ... gosh.

Julian T. Pettigrew was *not* pleased to see the visitors.

Don't touch that!

Hands off!

Get away from there!

The Binkertons *could* have stayed to help. But they were eager to get home to see their parents.

As the Binkertons walked away, they breathed a sigh of relief. This had been their toughest trip so far. They *never* wanted to see a Viking again for as long as they lived.

But never? Well, that's a very long time.

Even for time travelers.

THE VIKINGS

Fact or fantasy?

How much can you believe of *Adventures with the Vikings*?

The Binkerton kids are made up. Their adventures are made up, too. So the story of the Binkertons is just that — a story.

But there really were Vikings, who lived long ago and spent their time raiding, exploring, farming and ... well, if you really want to know, read the Guidebook! That's where you'll find the facts about the Vikings. All the information in Julian T. Pettigrew's Personal Guide to the Vikings is based on real historical facts.

More about the Vikings

For hundreds of years, the ancestors of the Vikings lived in the part of northern Europe we call Scandinavia. Then, around 800 A.D., the people in this area began a period of raiding, trading and exploration that lasted for 300 years (until about 1100 A.D.). They became known as Vikings, and we now think of this period of European history as the Age of the Vikings.

What made the Vikings leave their homes and travel to faraway lands? There are several possible reasons. Scholars believe that the population of Scandinavia was growing quickly at the beginning of the Viking Age, so that there was no longer enough good farm land to support everyone. At the same time, feuds and wars made life difficult for some Vikings, who believed they might have a better life somewhere else. Those looking for riches

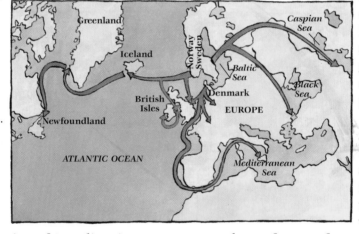

began to realize that there was unprotected wealth just a ship ride away, and their Viking longships made it possible to get there.

Although we use the term "Vikings" to refer to all Scandinavians of this time, there were actually three different Viking groups: Norwegians, Danes and Swedes.

The Norwegian Vikings raided the British Isles (including England, Scotland and Ireland) and islands in the north Atlantic. They sailed across the ocean to Iceland and Greenland, where they established settlements, and then even farther — to the coast of what is now Canada. Remains of a Viking settlement have been found in a place called L'Anse Aux Meadows in Newfoundland.

The Danish Vikings traveled south to carry on raids in Europe (in the countries now known as Belgium, France, Spain, Germany and the Netherlands). They also invaded England and conquered a large area called the Danelaw. Eventually, they ruled all of England for 26 years. In France, they (along with some Norwegian Vikings) gained control of an area still known as Normandy ("land of the North men").

The Swedish Vikings moved east and south toward the Caspian Sea and Black Sea. They built forts along the trade routes to the Middle East, where they traded with merchants from as far away as China and India.

Do we know everything about the Vikings? No! Will we learn more in future? Probably. Historians and archeologists never stop searching for new information about the past. They would love to time travel to the Age of the Vikings. If only they could find the right travel agency ...

In this book

The Vikings • 8
A Viking House • 10
Viking Society • 11
Viking Food • 12
Viking Work • 13
At Home with the Vikings • 15
Traveling by Land • 16

Viking Clothing • 17
A Viking Thing • 18
Viking Feuds and Punishments • 19
Viking Entertainment • 20
The Berserker • 21
A Viking Longship • 22
Viking Explorers and Settlers • 27

Life on a Viking Ship • 29
Viking Weapons and Armor • 30
A Viking Raid • 32
Viking Religion • 34
Viking Navigation • 35
Viking Towns and Trade • 41
The Viking Alphabet • 43